Mouthful of Forevers

CLEMENTINE VON RADICS

Andrews McMeel
Publishing®
a division of Andrews McMeel Universal

*For everyone who read these poems
before they were on these pages.
You are why this book exists.*

Contents

Change Came to Me
So Ugly Then

I Stopped Going to Therapy

Because I knew my therapist
was right, and I wanted
to keep being wrong.
I wanted to keep my bad habits
like charms on a bracelet.
I did not want to be brave.
I think I like my brain best
in a bar fight with my heart.
I think I like myself a little broken,
with rough edges, a little harder
to grasp. I like poetry
better than therapy anyway.
The poems never judge me
for healing wrong.

There Is the Worst
and Then There Is More

You silly little girl,
you think
you've survived so long
survival shouldn't hurt anymore.

You keep trying to turn
your body bulletproof.
You keep trying to turn your heart
bomb shelter.

Stop, darling.

You are soft and alive.
You bruise and heal. Cherish it.
It is what you were born to do.

It will not be beautiful,
but the truth never is.

Come now,
you promised yourself.
You promised
you'd live through this.

FOR THOSE LIKE ME, WITH HEARTS LIKE KINDLING

Darlings, sometimes love
will come to you like a fire
to a forest. When it does,
be braver than I was.

Just leave.

Take only what you can carry.
No tears, no second thoughts.
You have hands like tinder boxes,
the smallest spark will kill you.
Get in the car.

Take water to the maps.
Avoid gas stations. Don't look
at the flames dancing
in the rearview mirror.

Go to new cities,
climb on the rooftops and dance
with your coldest memories.
Wallpaper your new home
with every dusty,
desperate love letter you swore
you'd never send.

Find a stranger with sharp edges
and uncharted hips. Press your stories
into their skin and forget
you ever knew his name.

Just promise
you won't think of embers
or smoke.

Even when there is ash
in your hair.
Even when there is soot
in your lungs.

THAT SPRING EVERYTHING GREW WILD
AND THE RAIN CAME DOWN
LIKE PUNISHMENT

I sat on the fire escape
until the ashtrays were snowdrifts,
watching for storms on the horizon.
Begging the world for a reason
to lock all the doors.

Change came to me
so ugly then.
Showed up alone
with moldy suitcases
and too many demands, speaking
the language of hard looks
and wine headaches.
Telling me things I did not want
to know, growling,

Getting everything you ever wanted
does not make you want less

and

You break the hearts
of better people
who get in your way.

When will I stop belonging
to this hungry thing inside me?

What no one ever talks about
is how dangerous hope can be.
Call it forgiveness
with teeth.

I Pity the Woman Who
Will Love You When I Am Done

She will show up to your first date
with a dustpan and broom,
ready to pick up all the pieces
I left you in.
She will hear my name so often
it will begin to dig holes in her.
That is where doubt will grow.
She will look at your neck,
your thin hips, your mouth,
wondering at the ways
I touched you.
Offer you her lips, her throat,
the soft pillow of her thighs,
a sacrifice to the altar of virtue.
She will make you
all the promises I did
and some I never could.
She will hear only the terrible stories.
How I left you. How I lied.

She will wonder (as I have)
how someone as wonderful as you
could love a sinkhole like the woman
who came before her. Still,
she will compete with my ghost.
She will understand why
you do not look in the back of closets.
Why you are afraid of every groan
in the cold sweat of night.
She will know
every corner of you
is haunted by me.

MEDFORD, OREGON

We are from a place
like a thicket
of blackberry bushes.
Our home, this maze
of green snakes. Their fangs
an inevitability.
They scratch. Swell. Leaving
the most subtle kinds
of venom. No one
crawls out unscathed or without
crushed mouthfuls
of sugared fruit
in her stained, dripping
hand.
I say that
like I ever really left
at all.

On the Occasion of Our Anniversary

I.
This morning I googled
signs of domestic abuse
to remind myself I was right.
I still flinch at slamming doors,
a broken dish, a white couch.
There are days I yell so loud
I swear it's your voice
in my throat.

II.
I have learned
this world is the size of a fist,
lately an open palm. Whatever corner
you've got yourself chained up,
you will read this.

III.
Good.

The Poet Finally Drops the Bullshit

I am 15 and he is my first boyfriend. He is 18 and 6'4" and his hands are the size of thick textbooks. He says he has a lot to teach me. He is drowning in his own sadness. Drowning people often believe that if they grab hold of someone else they can be saved, but it just makes you both sink faster.

I am 17 and she is my first girlfriend. The only thing we do more than fight is fuck each other. I tell her about the boy's hands and she tries to stretch her fingers wide to mimic them. I say, *Stop it.* I say, *I love you as you are.*

I am 19 and in the first of many dirty rooms with books strewn everywhere and a mattress in one corner. These rooms always belong to boys with unshaved faces and tender hearts. Boys like this are a dime a dozen, but I don't know that yet because tonight I'm with the first one. He hands me a beer. He says he thinks I'm smart. He orders me to take off my clothes.

I am 20 and in love with someone who lies. The punishment for telling lies is being cruel. The punishment for being cruel is being abandoned.

I am 21 and it is not sex because I did not say yes. I say stop but that does not make it stop. I am 22 and crying because this new set of promises wants to kiss me, and I still taste like betrayal.

LEAVE HER LIPS
FOR SOME YOUNGER, PRETTIER GIRL

They ruby and burn,
stretch full over white teeth; taut
like a drum. I want her
to make music of me; instead
I water plants and envy their wet.
I wash dishes with unsteady hands.

Leave her hands to their work.
They are scarred with stories,
sliding thick down her legs as I stare.
Mouth cotton, thighs pulsing
to the steady rhythm
of her breath.
If I do not play this cool, she
could burn my house down.

Leave my house where it stands.
Let me have this. This crooked
home; the only person
who has ever promised not
to leave me. Let me be worthy
of the first good thing.

I am terrified
I will break his heart
just because I feel restless;
because it is between me
and what I hunger for.

Leave my hunger out of this.
It is stronger than any precaution.
My stomach drops tight
at her voice.
My palms itch
for her skin.
When she comes to me,
the closer she gets, the more
I want to give.
I want
to give her everything.

There Is a Lion in My Living Room

I feed it raw meat
so it does not hurt me.
It is a strange thing
to nourish what could kill you
in the hopes it does not kill you.
We have lived like this
for so many years.
Sometimes it feels like
we have always lived like this.
Sometimes I think
I have always been like this.

Here Is the Bitter Truth

That mouthful of thorns
you called our last kiss
still lingers
after so many others.

THOUGHTS ON CALIFORNIA

The summer I moved to Berkeley
in hopes of reinventing his smile,
the grapefruit tree in our yard
grew heavy with its own bounty.

I'd pick the sunbaked fruits
and split the pink flesh
with my bare hands
devouring it like a heart.

That was the summer
I wanted him to marry me so bad
I told everyone he asked when he didn't.
I'm not saying that's why I left.
The not saying does not make it
any quieter.

This Year

I'm not sure what to say about struggle except that it feels like a long, dark tunnel with no light at the end. You never notice until it's over the ways it has changed you, and there is no going back. We struggled a lot this year. For everyone who picked a fight with life and got the shit kicked out of them: I'm proud of you for surviving.

This year I learned that cities are beautiful from rooftops even when you're sad and that swimming in rivers while the sun sets in July will make you feel hopeful, no matter what's going on at home. I found out my best friend is strong enough to swing me over his shoulder like I'm weightless and run down the street while I'm squealing and kicking against his chest. I found out vegan rice milk whipped cream is delicious, especially when it's licked off the stomach of a boy you love.

This year I kissed too many people with broken hearts and hands like mousetraps. If I could go back and unhurt them I would. If I could go back even farther and never meet them I would do that too. I turned 21. There's no getting around it. I'm an adult now. Navigating the world has proved harder than I expected. There were times I was reckless. In my struggle to survive I hurt others. Apologies do not make good bandages.

I'm not sure what to say about change except that it reminds me of the Bible story with the lions' den. But you are not named Daniel and you have not been praying, so God lets the beasts get a few deep, painful swipes at you before the morning comes and you're pulled into the light, exhausted and cut to shit.

The good news is you survived. The bad news is you're hurt and no one can heal you but yourself. You just have to find a stiff drink and a clean needle before you bleed out. And then you get up. And start over.

THE BRIEF TWO SECONDS
AFTER YOU RUIN EVERYTHING

After your grandmother's
wedding ring
slides off your finger
and down the kitchen drain.

After your sister finally
unlocks her mouth and tells you
what happened the night
you didn't pick up the phone.

After that party
your freshman year of college
when you drank all the vodka
and threw yourself at that boy
who was so not into you.

After the picture frames,
the wineglass,
and your vows
lay broken on the floor.

After you drop out of college.

After your mother tells you
not to come home anymore.

After you accept that your father
and the man you love
have the same brown sugar eyes.

After it has been two years,
and you're still not sure
you love him.

After it has been four years,
and you're still not sure
you love him.

After he asks you to marry him,
and you're still not sure
you love him.

After you pull your underwear
from the dark curves
of a stranger's sheets
and leave
without saying good-bye.

After you, sobbing,
confess what you have done,
and he does not forgive you.

There is shame.
There is fear.
And there is this dizzying
freedom.

ALL THIS TIME

I drank you like the cure
when maybe
you were the poison.

Something is wrong.
There are flies over the bed.
Everything smells
like wasted blood.

We Call This Place Home

Three-Day Weekend

I.
If I had a shot of tequila
for every time I swore
I'd never drink again,
I'd be drowning in tequila.
When I get drunk all I do
is talk about you
and kiss boys who aren't you.
Our teeth clacking together,
empty bottles in a trash can.
That is exactly
what's wrong with me.

II.
After the bars close
we go behind the Safeway,
climb in the dumpsters,
and tear apart the trash bags
like raccoons. Pawing
through the salvageable,
feeling fish heads squish
under our boots.

You find a dozen
half-dead sunflowers
and present them to me
on bended knee.
Here, you say, *Finally,*
something as beautiful
as you are.

III.
The drunk pillow of your body
wraps around me
every night.
We built this crooked house
with our own shaking hands.
We call this place home.

You Have Six Tattoos

Full lips. Good, strong hands.
You have seven freckles
on your back;
they map out the Big Dipper.

You have a scar on your left arm
you carved there in high school.
The first time you pulled off
your T-shirt, I traced the line
with my fingers and fell in love
with your strength.

You are a hero for living
from that moment to this one.
You never need to apologize
for how you chose to survive.

Your body is a map
I know every inch of,
and if anyone else
were to kiss me,
all they would taste
is your name.

Three Tomatoes and a Mango

I'm learning how to tell stories
so I can tell the world your story.
I read poems but they fall short
of the way your hair falls across your face
so I shut the book. You have dirty hands
and a sugary heart and convenience store
taste in wine. The way you say my name
feels like fireworks on a strange day,
like October 9th or April 22nd.
This is a poem about the first time
I saw you naked and the night
you showed up at my door at 2 a.m.
with three tomatoes and a mango.
My calendar was rude enough to remind me
it's been 43 days since we last touched. Still,
I calculate how long it would take
to walk 2,387 miles
and strangely I feel better.
(598 hours. And 12 minutes.)

When He Asks Me to Describe Fear

I say my mother smelling vodka
on my breath at seventeen. I say grief
is a firework of blue left on the collarbone.
Superheroes always have broken hearts
and tragic backstories, so maybe I'm doing okay.
In my dreams we are brave enough
to leap tall buildings in a single bound,
and see through walls and also
never lie to each other.

Promise me this:
when you finally leave me, you'll get creative.
Tell me I was more disappointing
than your childhood. Send me your bloody ear
with a letter saying, *I've got to Gogh,*
you're making me crazy. I am hard to love
but know this much:
you are the only thing I like doing
more than writing poems.

ALL THAT'S LEFT TO TELL

I.
When I was trying
to quit smoking
and we drank white wine
from Mason jars,
you called my freckles
cocoa powder
and I called your green eyes
celery.

II.
I am learning how
to be a grown-up
who pays bills,
cooks her own meals,
and doesn't cry at words like
I think I just want to be friends.

III.
The truth is this:
Love is an organic thing.
It rots and softens.

FOR NIKKI

I know
you and I
are not about poems or
other sentimental bullshit
but I have to tell you
even the way
you drink your coffee
knocks me the fuck out.

SAME MOON

You told me mornings were the best time
to break your own heart. So here I am,
smoking your brand of cigarettes for the scent.
I wonder if you still sing Beatles songs
as you make coffee. You said your mother
used to sing them to you when you couldn't sleep,
nineteen years before we met, twenty
before you moved your clothes out of our closet
while I was at work. By the way, I hate you
for leaving all the photographs on the fridge.
Taking them down felt like peeling off new scabs,
like slapping a sunburn. I spent so many nights
carving your body into pillows, I can promise you
nothing feels like sleeping with your arm around me
and your breath in my ear. Still, it's comforting
to know we sleep under the same moon,
even if she's so much older when she gets to me.
I like to imagine she's seen you sleeping
and wants me to know you're doing well.

A Prayer

But to come home each night,
have a drink, go to bed,
and be so deeply understood by you
would be the greatest gift of my life.

3 Beers In

It's 11 a.m. and I'm sitting in a restaurant
3 beers in. Believe me, even I'm surprised
I'm still alive sometimes. I have been
drinking about you for 2 days. Lately
you remind me of a wild thing, chewing
through its foot. But you are already free
and I don't know what to do
except trace the rough line of your jaw
and try not to place blame. Here is the truth:
It is hard to be in love with someone
who is in love with someone else.
I don't know how to turn that into poetry.

October

I thought leaving you would be easy,
just walking out the door. But I keep
getting pinned against it with my legs
around your waist and it's like
my lips want you like my lungs want air;
it's just what they were born to do.
So I am sitting at work thinking of you
cutting vegetables in my kitchen.
Your hair in my shower drain.
Your fingers on my spine in the morning
while we listen to Muddy Waters.
I don't know why I've got so much hope
pinned to someone who will never call me
home, but the way you talk about poems
like Marxists talk of revolution,
it makes me want to keep trying.
In the mornings, in my shower drain,
in the music, in the walk out the door.
I am looking for reasons to love you.
I am looking for proof that you love me.

You Draw Constellations in My Freckles

I mean you ask me
not to fall in love with you
and then you go write poems
with your tongue
and draw constellations
in my freckles.

Advice to Teenage Girls with Wild Ambitions and Trembling Hearts

When you are 13 years old,
the heat will be turned up too high
and the stars will not be in your favor.
You will hide behind a bookcase
with your family and everything hunted.
You will spend years pouring an ocean
into a diary. When they find you,
they will treat you like nothing more
than a spark above a burning bush.
Still, tell them,
Despite everything,
I really believe people are good at heart.

When you are 14 years old,
a voice will call you to greatness.
When the doubters call you crazy,
do not listen. They don't know the sound
of their own God's whisper.
Do not let their doubting drown out
the sound of your own heartbeat.
You are the Maid of Untamed Patriotism.
You were born to lead armies
and unite a nation like a broken heart.

When you are 15 years old,
you will be punished
for learning too proudly.
A man will climb onto your school bus
and insist your sisters name you enemy.
When you do not hide, he will point his gun
and fire three times. Three years later,
in an ocean of survival, and no apologies,
you will stand before the leaders
of the world and tell them
how your country is burning.

When you are 16 years old,
you will invent science fiction.
The story of a man named Frankenstein
and his creation. You will soon learn
young girls with big ideas
are far more terrifying than monsters,
but don't be afraid. You will be remembered
long after they have put down their torches.

When you are 17 years old,
you will strike out Babe Ruth
then Lou Gehrig, one right after the other.
Grown men will be so afraid of the lightning
in your fingertips that a few days later
all women will be fired
from the major leagues. The reason?
Girls are too delicate to play baseball.

You will turn 18
with a baby on your back,
leading Lewis and Clark
across North America.

You will turn 18
and be queen of the Nile.

You will turn 18
and bring justice to journalism.

You are now 18,
standing on the precipice,
trembling before your own greatness.

This is your call to leap.

There will always be those
who say you are too young and delicate
to make anything happen for yourself.
They don't see the part of you that smolders.
Don't let their doubting drown out
the sound of your own heartbeat.

You are the first drop of rain in a hurricane.

Your bravery builds beyond you.
You are needed by all the little girls
still living in secret, writing oceans
made of monsters, and
throwing like lightning.
You don't need to grow up
to find greatness.

You are so much stronger than the world
has ever believed you could be.
The world is waiting for you
to set it on fire. Trust in yourself

and burn.

Love Poems

I want to kiss you.
Like big, fat kisses. Or angels. Or stars.
Or something. I don't know.
Love poems never make sense to me.
Poets say things like
Your teeth are flowers
or *Your eyes are miracles.* But you
aren't miracles. Or flowers.
You are some sweet boy with a good smile
and a shaky heart. Come kiss me.
I'm in love with the miracle of your body—
beside my body.

I Am Jealous of Your Tattoos

And how long
they will stay with you
after I go.

Poem for My Mother When She Doesn't Feel Beautiful

Don't worry about your body.
It isn't as small as it once was
but honestly, the world
needs more of you.
You look in the mirror
like you've done something wrong
but you look perfect.
Anyone who says otherwise
is telling you a lie
to make you feel weak
and you know better.
You have survived every day
for as long as you've been alive.
You could spit fire if you wanted.

My Father Sits Me Down to Teach Me How to Play Guitar

First off, he tells me,
your fingers are going to blister.
Your fingers are going to bleed.

Here: Let's start with the D chord.
This is how you play *Down on the Bayou*.
Vibrations travel through the body,
and that is how sound is made.

Here: This is how I pray.
These are the notes that roughly translate
to *Hallelujah*. This is how you play
I Won't Back Down. Now,
Don't Back Down.

Every song has a rhythm
you have to find like a pulse.
The beauty of music
is you are never done learning.
There is always time to get better.

Clementine, you have to push harder
with your fingers! You have to be stronger
than this.

Here: This is how I mourn.
How I take revenge and tell stories,
ask the woman I love to dance with me.
This is how I built our family.
This is how I built our home.

Here: This is the heartbeat
of the song you were named for.

Have I ever told you
why your name is Clementine?

The first time I held you
all I could think was, *Oh my darlin',*
Oh my darlin'.

Oh my darlin', it is time you learn
everything worth loving
takes hard work and patience.

See, I know you.
You are the good half of me.
People like us are not good with words.
What we mean gets muddled and wrong
somewhere between our minds
and our mouths.

We make art to say how we feel.

Here: These are the chords
to *Make You Feel My Love.*

Morning Haiku

You've no idea
how I want to be the blood
pumping through your heart.

Nothing to Close a Door

MERMAID

The day I surrendered to my limp,
and went out and bought my cane,
I realized I was done with the burden
of having feet.

Instead,
I am going to become a mermaid.
If everyone is going to stare at me, at least
let it be because I'm beautiful.

Besides,
I have always liked the ocean,
the promise of depth. I am tired
of this dry world, with all of its dust
and sickness, these barren fields.
I want to dive without drowning.
I want to swim among the teeth.
I want to braid my hair with seaweed
and mythology. I want men to carve me
into the bows of their ships
like a prayer, before I lure them
into the depths with my fishnet mouth.

I want the beauty,
the gorgeous mutation, the legend
of half body. All the wisdom of a woman
without the failures of sex. I am plunging.
I am sinking. I am not coming up for air.

I do not want all this human.

My legs move
like they resent being legs; my body
is wrecked by all this gravity.
I cannot face another morning waking up
with no hope of a fairytale.

Here on land, I cannot move.
Here on land, I cannot breathe.
On land, I am always drowning.
I am always drowning.

It's the Way

Every poem is about you.
Even the ones about other people,
they're for your eyes only.
Everyone else who reads them
is just a stranger
looking through the window at us.
It always comes back to you. It will always
come back to you. It's the way
I love you through literature.
I gave you a book about journeys
before you left. Do you remember?
And one about home. I filled it with notes,
instructions on how to miss me.
I was afraid you wouldn't know how,
and you'd give up.
Frustrated.

THE WEDDING

Tell me again about the wedding
we did not have. How I did not wear white,
did not choke on tradition, did not blush.
All the weddings that were not weddings.
The vows that were just sneezing.
The road ahead painted on a wall and how
we sped over and over again into the brick.
I say *we*. Like you weren't just standing there,
watching me bruise.

Did you know I built us a home,
laid the brick, filled it with Jameson
and apple-cheeked children?
I tried to slip the key onto your tongue
but you cannot kiss a smile.
So my home is not an honest home.
So my home is an empty bed.
That's the thing about heartbreak.
It's the smallest of worlds ending.
Everyone goes around you smiling,
like it's nothing to close a door.

Notes on the Faces of Monsters

I'm afraid of a lot of things.
None of them are the boogeyman.

That creature is waiting under your bed
to meet you when the lights are off.
When the most hideous parts of them
aren't obvious right away.

I get that, boogeyman. I can relate.

Things I am afraid of
are a lot more common.
Gaining weight, a grown man crying,
any article about an abuse survivor
that contains the words
It still affects my current relationships.

I fear a story
in which a stubborn wound
does not stay stitched, but rips open
with the flex of muscle.

Once a man
(who was barely not a boy)
gave me pills until I could not speak
then did what he did
with my lack of language.
I am afraid he crawled inside me
and never really left my body.

I picture him waiting,
crouched in my throat
for the moment I am most in love
to reach his hands back out
and strike again.

On Being a Writer

Look at us,
smiling with all our teeth out.
Suffering so bravely in the spotlight,
spilling blood on the page.
Behind the curtain
someone is bleeding.
There is dust on the floor.
You can smell the mold.

IF ASKED TO DESCRIBE HIM

I would tell them he is the twelfth time I tried to quit smoking. I would tell them he is the spark that burns the forest down. I would tell them he is the forest. I would tell them he is pulled teeth. I would tell them he is a barking dog. I would tell them he is never lonely, which is terrifying. I would tell them he is late-night talk of broken windows. I would tell them silver is still silver, even when it is blackened. I would tell them I have done my research, and love is not a state of being. It is a house that takes up the whole world. I would tell them I am everywhere except apart from him.

How We Heal

Things I Do When I Cannot Hold You

Buy all your favorite foods
so I will be ready when you come home
because once I did that and you said,
This is how I know you love me.

Go on long walks alone.

Think about a poem
my friend wrote that goes,
This is how you die by distance.

Hum the sound of the dial tone
under my breath.

Stare at my hands
and wonder at their uses.
Think of pawning my thighs.
Consider auctioning off my hipbones.
Place my breasts in a box
on the top shelf of the closet.
I do not need them now.

Roll every story I have to give you
like a marble on my tongue,
terrified to choke or swallow.

Stories like:

Baby,
I just found out pumpkins
are technically fruit!

and

Darling!
Cary Grant's first job
was in a traveling circus

and

Love,
most mammals
are born able to walk
and learn to run within minutes,
so we are not crazy
for moving so fast.

This morning I wrote your name
in the steam on my mirror,
knowing full well
it would fade within minutes.

In my best notebook
I wrote, *I Miss You I Miss You,*
ten thousand times.

I wrote, *I am definitely missing
one of my ribs.*

I wrote, *I envy the way leaves
know exactly when to fall from the branches
and when to come back
in the spring.*

I wrote, *Everyone else isn't you.
It turns out that's a huge problem for me.*

Here Is What I Know

You drink your coffee black and we
are afraid of each other. Once
you kissed my neck in front of your friends
and it made me very shy.
Once you kissed my stomach
and I started crying.
I see the tender way you touch things
and want to kiss your nose
but I keep my mouth to myself.
Your collarbones are craters
big enough to fit my fist into.
You are the most beautiful thing
I have seen in months. I was not good
to the last person I loved
so I punished my heart
(I let it break and bleed out
then roughly sewed it back together).
It is hard to write poems
when I only know how to fuck you.
I am always trying.
I am thinking of Somedays.
I am saying Good-bye. You asked why
I never write anything honest
so I am writing you this.

The First Time
You Washed Up at Our Door

After a night of out-swimming
your own ghosts, I was seven years old.
You smelled like something sour.
The jagged, bleeding zipper
of your mouth split open
like a Halloween mask.

You healed beautifully,
swore you were dry.
Lasted 30 days and showed up again,
spilling over our porch, sobriety chips
still sloshing in your pocket.

Each year that passed
has brought you a new set of scars.
You don't even look like a man anymore.
More like a warning. A car wrapped
around a telephone pole,
an animal limping along the edge
of the highway. The lighthouse,
its huge, single eye
warning of storms, screaming,
Turn around, go.
There is no harbor here.

Tonight you are in a hospital
somewhere south of me.
A machine is forcing life into a heart
you have been trying to drown
my whole life.

I am sorry I haven't visited.
I know I haven't called. I don't know
why this business of living
is so much harder for you.

This morning I saw a bottle
thrown from a car.
The glass shattered
in a dangerous, glittering
explosion. Staining the grit
and the cracks of the sidewalk,
a mosaic of beautiful,
senseless destruction.

On Healing

I have been told that when
someone dies, the worst part
is not the blood, or the shock,
or the long days after,
where some child in you believes
they are not really gone.

No,
the worst part comes later.
When the world heals you too well
and you begin to forget their face.
After grief has found another home
and their voice is a song
for which you cannot remember the tune.

I don't have this problem of forgetting.
I remember your face exactly.
Your voice is right here
coloring my voice. Nothing is helping me
forget your hands, how they shook
like apologizing mountains
hollowed in suffering.

I don't know about the part
where you cannot remember grief.
Grief comes for me every morning,
dragging everything I never told you
behind him like screaming children.

You are not gone. Your hands
are in my hands.
Your eyes are somewhere
in my eyes. Everything I see now
is another thing you'll never see.

When I Was Seven Years Old

We adopted a dog
who ran away two weeks later,
back to the home of the man
who didn't want her.

We found her there,
howling at the darkened windows.
No one lived there anymore.
All the doors were locked. Dogs
are so disappointing in their loyalty
to the wrong things.

All of this is to say
I'm having the kind of afternoon
where I break a dish
and stand over the kitchen sink
for hours, staring
at the two irreparable halves.

There is no longer
a woman in my body.

Just this screaming child
who does not listen.
She only wants.
And wants. And wants.
Stubborn in her devotion.

And he is still gone.
And grief is a swamp that sinks
much deeper than you'd expect.

And I am still here.
I still remember him.

The Story Behind Lobsters

Is that they weren't considered
a delicacy until the 19th century.
Before that they were peasant food,
most often served in prisons.

The story behind diamonds
is they were just rocks until 1938,
when a marketing campaign
forever linked them with love.

The story behind art
is that it is never a masterpiece
until it has been bought and hung
on the wall in someone
else's home.

The story behind us
is until I lost you
I had no idea
what you were worth.

Untitled 1

When he says you love too deeply,
remind him he was warned.

When no one else is awake,
don't call him.

When the poems don't come,
don't open the vodka.

When the poems don't come,
go to sleep.

When you wake up from
the wanting,
go back to sleep.

When he shows up in
your nightmares,
don't offer your forgiveness.

When he offers you his lips,
go for the throat.

The Ways I Didn't Leave You

Even though I knew how it felt
to love someone with a heart
like the sharp edge of a knife,
I pulled out the whetstone.

I asked you to bend,
to be small enough to close my fist
around. I wanted to be certain
you could never get away.

I knew there was someone else,
but I started looking through your pockets
for proof I was wrong.

I threw a wineglass across the kitchen
like a fastball; we both stood and stared
at the shattered glass, proof
that good people do terrible things.

I said, *I love you*
when I meant something much
more specific, I should have said,
Please don't leave me,
I'm afraid to sleep alone.

Hard Morning

In the airport bathroom mirror my face
is not the one I recognize. It's harsher. Older.
I'm 22 and I have a wrinkle above my nose.
I don't like this evidence that I'm going to die
reflected back at me. I don't like that I care more
about phone calls than headlines.
I don't like the way your smile is an exit wound.
Maybe you are a mistake I made young.
Maybe you are unprotected sex. A bad haircut.
Maybe I won't walk through life with a rock
in my boot. Maybe the sun will explode
and the moon will fly out of orbit.
Maybe I will burn so fast
there won't even be time to think of you
once more.

Untitled 2

What doesn't kill you leaves disfiguring scars

What doesn't kill you fills you
with paralyzing self-hatred

What doesn't kill you makes you an unfit mother

What doesn't kill you makes it all so hard

What doesn't kill you wakes you up
in the middle of the night

What doesn't kill you turns you into an alcoholic

What doesn't kill you makes you do unforgivable things
to the people you love

What doesn't kill you makes you afraid
for the rest of your life

What doesn't kill you might make you kill them

The Difference

Between being loved
and being fucked
is I can't remember how the first feels.
I have a body like an open door.
I have a body like an open hand.
It is too easy to hold me.

Find me a boy
with a heart more hopeful
than spun sugar on a hot day;
I will teach him to render me
meaningless.

The whole time,
every moment,
wishing he'd crack me open,
rib by rib, to see how I work.
How I bleed.

PAPER BODY

I wonder if you know yet
that you'll leave me.
That you are a child
playing with matches
and I have a paper body.
You will meet a girl
with a softer voice
and stronger arms and she
will not have violent secrets
or an affection for red wine
or eyes that never stay dry.
You will fall into her bed
and I'll go back
to spending Friday nights with boys
who never learn my last name.

I have chased off every fool
who has tried to sleep beside me.
You think it's romantic to fuck the girl
who writes poems about you.
You think I'll understand your sadness
because I live inside my own.

But I will show up at your door
at 2 a.m., wild-eyed and sleepless,
trying to find some semblance of peace
in your breastbone
and you will not let me in.
You will tell me to go home.

But My Heart

Is an old house
(the kind my mother
grew up in)
hell to heat and cool
and faulty in the wiring
and though it's nice to look at
I have no business
inviting others in.

Every Time a Man Yells

I am seven years old again
and he is packing that suitcase
once more.

Picking me up by the neck,
teaching me obedience.

To be soft,
like the belly of a fish
exposed to a knife.

It's Just So Strange

He used to love me,
and now
he's just a stranger
who happens to know
all my secrets.

Untitled 3

Be merciful until you can't be.
Until you feel your heart begin to harden
into a bullet.

Then use that bullet.

Salome Redux

Salome dances her dance
of the seven veils;
the men all eye her
like wolves on the hunt,
this beautiful girl
finally undressing for them.
Finally they can see her
exactly as they want to.

The first veil drops.

In 2007, Kim Kardashian's ex-boyfriend
released their sex tape against her will.
Kim Kardashian, rather than hide in shame,
used the publicity to promote her own career.

Salome
moves like a dream
half-remembered.
Salome dances
like a siren song.
All the men ache to see
the hot sugar
of her hip bones.

The second veil drops.

In 2014, Kim Kardashian walks down the aisle
as the whole world watches. If only all of us
were so successful in our revenge.
If only all of us stood in our Louboutin heels
on the backs of the men who betray us,
surveying the world we created for ourselves.

The third veil drops.

Kim Kardashian knows exactly what you think of her.
She presses the cloth tighter against her skin.
Her smile is a promise she never intends to keep.

Salome shows us her body
but never her eyes.

The fourth veil drops.

The four things most recently tweeted
at Kim Kardashian were:

@KimKardashian Suck My Dick
@KimKardashian Can I Meet Kanye?
@KimKardashian Please Fuck Me
@KimKardashian I Love You. I Love You.

Women are told
to keep their legs shut.
Women are told
to keep their mouths shut.
Some women are kept silent
for so long they become experts
in the silent theft of power.

The fifth veil has dropped.

Kim Kardashian made 12 million dollars this year.
Yesterday, uncountable men in their miserable jobs
told their miserable friends that Kim was nothing
but a *dumb whore*. Kim Kardashian will never
even learn their names.

The sixth veil has dropped.

The seventh veil has dropped.

And Salome sat beside King Herod.
And he swore unto her,
"Whatsoever thou shalt ask of me,
I will give to thee
unto the half of my kingdom."
And she smiled, and said,
"Bring me the head
of John the Baptist.
Punish the man who hurt me."

I Read Her Palms Naked in Bed

White sheets covering our breasts
and rolling stomachs, shy again
now that the storms of moaning
have passed. I point to her life line,
explain how each crease is a time
she has overcome something.
She laughs, throwing her head back,
letting her hair shake down
her shoulders, exposing
the long column of her throat.
A perfect stretch of canvas.

The warmth of her hand in my hand
is so sweet it makes me dizzy.
I cannot believe her when she says
I am beautiful. She cannot want me,
not the way I want her. My want
is an Empire State Building
I monster-climb with her
clutched in my fist. They make old,
flickering horror movies
about the way I look at her mouth.

It is not a secret
that other women terrify me.
We are always competing in a contest
I don't understand.
I don't know how to beautiful.
I don't know how to gentle.
There is a right way to be this gender.
It has been taught to me
since birth.
I have failed every class.

Cleopatra's Palace
as an Elaborate Metaphor
for Why I Didn't Call Him Back

I.
When I think of love, I
think of a snakebite
to the chest.

II.
He was right.
Uncountable lifetimes ago
there was an empire in Egypt.
But we burned the libraries.
We destroyed the temples.
Everything that was beautiful then
is lost to us now.

III.
These days poetry
is the only language
I know how to speak.
But he speaks anthropology.
He speaks hieroglyphs. He
spends his life studying things
I can only bury
in metaphors.

IV.
My body
is a war-weathered monument
to the desert.

V.
My chest
is the stone tomb
inside it.

VI.
Our vows,
a book of prayers I buried
with the dead.

VII.
Last year they found
Cleopatra's palace sunk deep
in the Mediterranean Sea
They are going to build
a museum.

You and I both know
anything they could learn
from the ruins
of her once home
is not worth
emptying oceans for.

SOMEDAY I WILL STOP BEING YOUNG AND WANTING STUPID TATTOOS

There are seven people in my house;
we each have different genders.
I cut my hair over the bathroom sink
and everything I own is dirty.
We sit around the kitchen table
and argue about the compost pile,
and Karl Marx, and the necessity
of violence when The Rev comes
(whatever the fuck *The Rev* means).

There is a river
running through this city and
every time my best friend laughs
I want to grab him by the shoulders
and shout *Grow old with me*
and never kiss me on the mouth!
I want to spend the next eighty years
together, eating Doritos
and riding bikes.

I want to be Oscar the Grouch.
I want him and his girlfriend
to be Bert and Ernie. We can live
on Sesame Street. I will park
my trash can on their front stoop
and we can be best friends every day.
If I ever seem grouchy,
I'm just a little afraid of all that fun.

There is a river
running through this city I know
as well as my own name.

It is the first place to ever call my heart home.
It is not poetry
to be in love with the water.
It is not naive to love what creates you.
It is not blasphemy
to see God in the skyline.

I have built my family
of these buildings and these people.

There is always cold beer
asking to be slurped on back porches.
There are always crushed packs
of American Spirits in my back pocket.
I have been wearing
the same jeans for ten days.

Someday
I will stop being young
and wanting stupid tattoos.

DESIRE

God I want you
in some primal, wild way
animals want each other.
Untamed and full of teeth.

God I want you
in some chaste, Victorian way.
A glimpse of your ankle
just kills me.

Mouthful of Forevers

I am not the first person you loved.
You are not the first person I looked at
with a mouthful of forevers. We
have both known loss like the sharp edges
of a knife. We have both lived with lips
more scar tissue than skin. Our love came
unannounced in the middle of the night.
Our love came when we'd given up
on asking love to come. I think
that has to be part
of its miracle.

This is how we heal.
I will kiss you like forgiveness. You
will hold me like I'm hope. Our arms
will bandage and we will press promises
between us like flowers in a book.
I will write sonnets to the salt of sweat
on your skin. I will write novels to the scar
on your nose. I will write a dictionary
of all the words I have used trying
to describe the way it feels to have finally,
finally found you.

And I will not be afraid
of your scars.

I know sometimes
it's still hard to let me see you
in all your cracked perfection,
but please know:
Whether it's the days you burn
more brilliant than the sun
or the nights you collapse into my lap,
your body broken into a thousand questions,
you are the most beautiful thing I've ever seen.
I will love you when you are a still day.
I will love you when you are a hurricane.

LOLITA ADDRESSES HER AUTHOR

Maybe you wanted to make a monster.
The story of a man destroyed by his own desires,
a snake swallowing a mouse whole.
Maybe you didn't know how it feels
the way a man stares at a little girl's legs
like they're lollipop sticks.
Like her sugar cube body
would melt in his mouth.
Maybe you don't know then how it feels
to be devoured. To open your bed
and find the Big Bad Wolf
in your mother's clothes.

Maybe you've never seen a child
asking for attention in a language
she does not know how to speak.
Opening the softest, warmest
parts of her, asking for love
the only way she knows how.

But instead,
all I am is what he made me.
Grown men spit out *Lolita*
as another word for *asking for it*.
Little girls playing at women,
red lipstick clacking like a lollipop
against their teeth. Children
read my story like a fairytale.
How can I forgive you
for turning me into the poison
other daughters learn to swallow?
Mr. Vladimir, you set out
to create a monster,
but you created the wrong one.

Poem for the Girl
Who Texted My Boyfriend
in the Middle of the Night

You pretty little scorpion
on his nightstand. You mosquito

flying into our bedroom,
carrying all your bloody threats.

Your lack of sickness,
your threat of sting.

Imagine me a frog, long tongue
slithering out to swallow you

whole. Imagine him, warm, asleep
beside me. While you wait

for his response, phone poised
in your hand like a rattlesnake.

NEEDLE

Inside me are a lot of people,
most of them good.
Somewhere inside me
is the girl that loved you.
You did things to me
you should not have done.
Because of that I was less a girl.
Because of that I called what you did love.
That is what children often do.
The needle that goes through
leaves behind a thread.
And maybe that is love,
in the sense that love
has too many definitions.

Index

Acknowledgments

Thank you to Portland and the strange family that lives here. Thank you to Eric and Elizabeth von Radics, for being my parents and having seemingly endless patience and support. To Ellie, Maya, and Skylar: In my heart you are all my little sisters. Thank you to Kiki, Meggie, Fortesa, Kristina, and the rest of the beautiful Where Are You Press women. Thank you to Grace Suh and Andrews McMeel. Thank you to Chris Leja and Caitlyn Seihl and the Portland Poetry Slam for lending your brilliance and making this book better. Thank you, Alex, always, for being my home.

About the Author

Clementine von Radics was born in Alameda, California. She has toured two continents performing her poetry and is the founder of Where Are You Press, a publishing house that focuses on the voices of young women. She has taught and performed poetry in warehouses, church basements, and correctional facilities. She lives in Portland, Oregon, where it always smells like rain.

Andrews McMeel Publishing
a division of Andrews McMeel Universal
1130 Walnut Street, Kansas City, Missouri 64106

www.andrewsmcmeel.com

16 17 18 19 20 RR4 10 9 8 7 6 5 4

ISBN: 978-1-4494-7079-1

Library of Congress Control Number: 2014959866

Editor: Grace Suh
Art Director: Holly Ogden
Production Editor: Erika Kuster
Production Manager: Carol Coe

Photo credit (back cover): Jasmine Sennhauser

Attention: Schools and Businesses
Andrews McMeel books are available at quantity discounts
with bulk purchase for educational, business, or sales promotional use.
For information, please e-mail the Andrews McMeel Special Sales Department:
specialsales@amuniversal.com.